Bugs Are Beautiful!

A+ books

MAGNIFICENT Moths

by Martha E. H. Rustad

Consultant:
Laura Jesse
Director, Plant and Insect Diagnostic Clinic
Iowa State University Extension
Ames, Iowa

• • •

CAPSTONE PRESS
a capstone imprint

A+ Books are published by Capstone Press
1710 Roe Crest Drive, North Mankato, Minnesota 56003
www.mycapstone.com

Library of Congress Cataloging-in-Publication Data
Names: Rustad, Martha E. H. (Martha Elizabeth Hillman), 1975- author.
Title: Magnificent moths / by Martha E. H. Rustad.
Description: North Mankato, Minnesota : Capstone Press, [2017] | Series: Bugs are beautiful! | Series: A+ books |
Audience: Ages 4-8. | Audience: K to grade 3. | Includes bibliographical references and index.
Identifiers: LCCN 2016032404 (print) | LCCN 2016041176 (ebook) | ISBN 9781515744993 (library binding) |
ISBN 9781515745037 (pbk.) | ISBN 9781515745150 (eBook PDF)
Subjects: LCSH: Moths–Juvenile literature.
Classification: LCC QL544.2 .R878 2017 (print) | LCC QL544.2 (ebook) | DDC 595.78–dc23
LC record available at https://lccn.loc.gov/2016032404

J
595.78
Rus

Editorial Credits
Editor, Abby Colich; Designer, Bobbie Nuytten; Media Researcher, Jo Miller; Production Specialist, Tori Abraham

Photo Credits
Glow Images: Prisma RM/Schwab Lukas, 18; Minden Pictures: Robert Thompson, 20; National Geographic
Creative: George Grall, 25; Newscom: Bulten-beeld/Klaas van Haeringen, 28, imageBROKER/FLPA/Malcolm
Schuyl, 29, imageBROKER/Hans Lang, 19, Photoshot/NHPA/Robert Pickett, 27 (top); Science Source: E.R.
Degginger, 26, John Serrao, 21, Michael P. Gadomski, 13; Shutterstock: blewulis, 4, Bonnie Taylor Barry, 6,
BOONCHUAY PROMJIAM, 27 (bottom), Brian Lasenby, 22, Cathy Keifer, cover, 7, 23, Cathy Keifer, 30 (eggs, molt,
adult), hwongcc, 16, IanRedding, 5 (top), Jacques VANNI, 11, Joseph Calev, 12, Marek R. Swadzba, 15, Matt
Jeppson, 30 (caterpillars, cocoon), Melinda Fawver, 5 (bottom), Mogens Trolle, 10, Oleksander Berezko, 14, Orapin
Joyphuem, 17, PKZ, 9, Puwadol Jaturawutthichai, map (throughout), Randimal, 8, RODINA OLENA, back cover
(background), StevenRusselSmithPhotos, 24, tony mills, 1

Note to Parents, Teachers, and Librarians

This Bugs Are Beautiful book uses full-color photographs and a nonfiction
format to introduce the concept of moths. Bugs Are Beautiful is designed
to be read aloud to a pre-reader or to be read independently by an early
reader. Photographs help listeners and early readers understand the text and
concepts discussed. The book encourages further learning by including the
following sections: Table of Contents, Glossary, Read More, Internet Sites,
Critical Thinking Using the Common Core, and Index. Early readers may need
assistance using these features.

Printed and bound in China.
007882

Table of Contents

Moths Are **Magnificent!**

Look at that insect fly by. Watch it land on its six legs. Can you see its hairy body? Its two antennae perk up. The antennae let the bug smell and feel. Two pairs of wings spread out wide. Wow! The wings are bright and colorful. This bug is a moth. Moths are magnificent.

Cecropia Moth

RANGE: Parts of the United States and Canada

WINGSPAN: 6 inches (15 centimeters)

MAGNIFICENT FEATURE: Patterns on wings and body

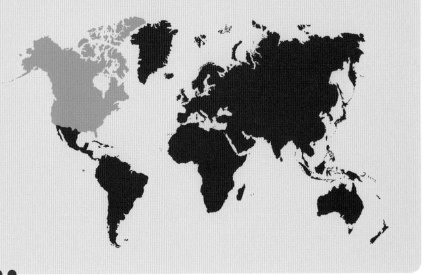

Check out the markings on the cecropia moth. This moth is bright orange, brown, and white. Its thick, fuzzy body has stripes and spots. As caterpillars they eat and molt. Then they spin a cocoon.

Adults do not eat. They live for only two weeks. They mate and lay eggs. Then they die.

Cinnabar Moth

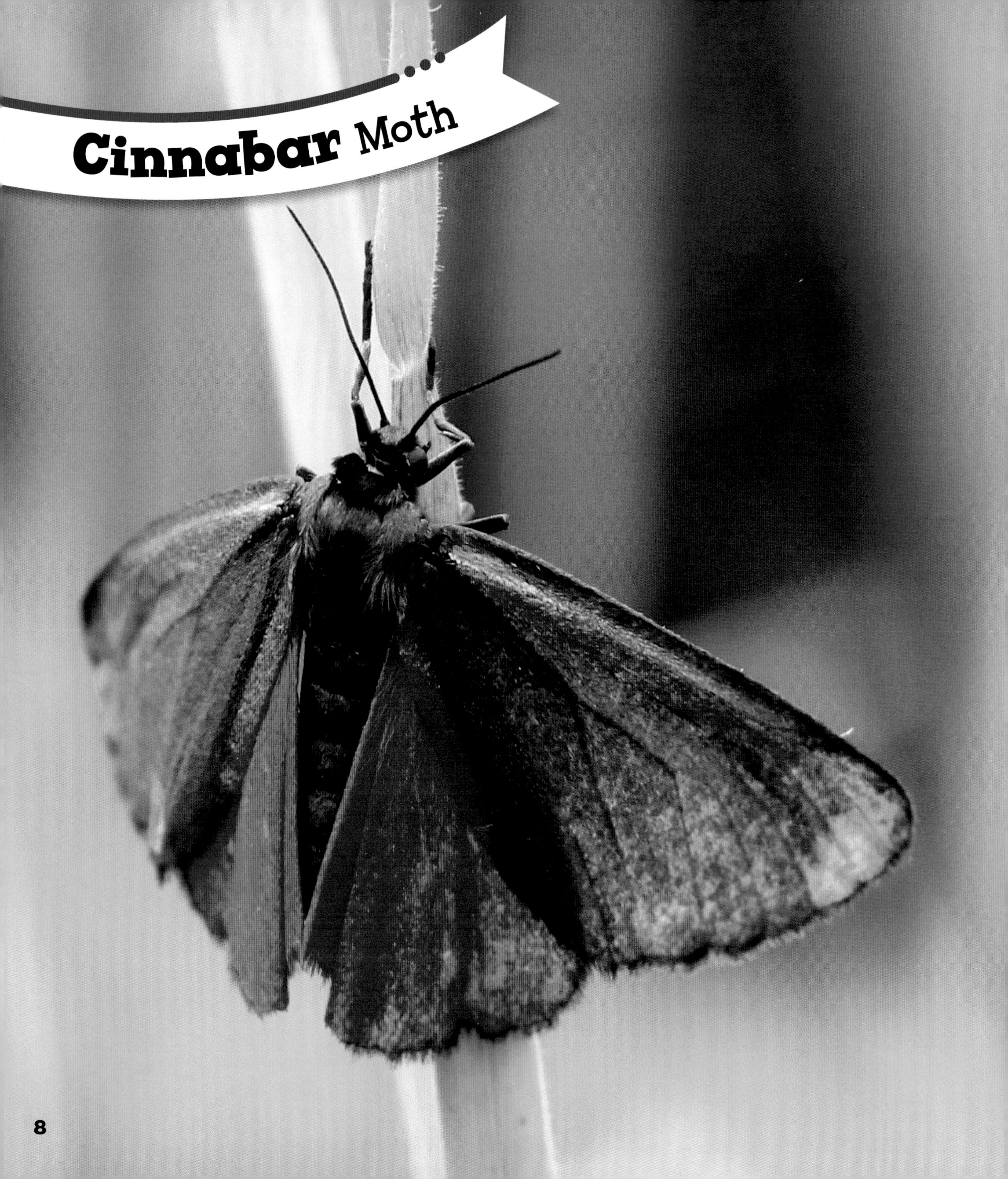

RANGE: Europe and Asia

WINGSPAN: 1.5 inches (4 cm)

MAGNIFICENT COLORS: Black and red

Are you seeing red? The red on the cinnabar moth is a warning. The bright color tells hungry predators to stay away. Why? As a caterpillar, the moth eats ragwort. Ragwort is a poisonous flower. The poison doesn't hurt the moth. It stays inside its body as it grows. It makes the adult moth taste badly to other animals.

caterpillar

Comet Moth

eyespots

RANGE: Madagascar

WINGSPAN: 8 inches (20 cm)

MAGNIFICENT FEATURE: Long wing tails

Are those eyes? The comet moth has one spot on each wing. The spots look like big eyes to hungry predators. The "eyes" scare predators away.

The comet moth is one of the world's largest. Its hind wings have long red tails. A male's tails can reach 6 inches (15 cm) long. A female's are shorter.

Isabella Tiger Moth

woolly bear caterpillar

RANGE: North America

WINGSPAN: 1 inch (2.5 cm)

MAGNIFICENT SKILL: Caterpillars survive being frozen

Brrr! Caterpillars of the isabella tiger moth survive the cold! Adults lay eggs in summer. Woolly bear caterpillars hatch. All summer and fall, they eat and grow. Cold winter comes. The caterpillars freeze solid! In spring they thaw. Then they eat more. Soon they spin cocoons. They stay in the cocoons for two weeks. Then adult moths break out.

Jersey Tiger Moth

RANGE: Europe

WINGSPAN: 2.5 inches (6.4 cm)

MAGNIFICENT FEATURE: Different looking pairs of wings

A Jersey tiger moth is sipping nectar. A hungry bird is near. The bird sees the moth's black and white wings. The pattern confuses the bird. Then the moth flashes its orange hind wings. The bird sees the orange and stays away. It knows the moth will taste badly. Both pairs of the moth's wings look very different. The colors in both pairs keep it safe.

Oleander Hawk Moth

16

RANGE: Europe, Africa, Middle East, Southern Asia

WINGSPAN: 5 inches (13 cm)

MAGNIFICENT COLORS: Many shades of green

eyespots on caterpillar

This moth has its own camouflage! The Oleander hawk moth is many shades of green. Some call it the army green moth. Its pattern helps the moth hide among plants. Caterpillars are green. They have two green and black spots. The spots look like eyes.

Peppered Moth

Can you see the moths on this tree? Peppered moths are black and white. Some are mostly black. Their colors blend in with dark tree trunks. Other peppered moths are mostly white. Their colors help them hide on light tree trunks. Caterpillars also use camouflage. They look like twigs. Hungry predators can't see them on trees.

RANGE: North America, Europe, Asia

WINGSPAN: 2.5 inches (6.4 cm)

MAGNIFICENT FEATURE: Camouflage

Can you spot the caterpillar?

Polka Dot Wasp Moth

RANGE: Southeastern United States, Caribbean Islands, Central America

WINGSPAN: 2 inches (5 cm)

MAGNIFICENT FEATURE: Looks like a wasp

Is that a wasp? No. This shiny blue insect is a moth. White spots cover its body. The tip of its body is red. Predators fear this moth. They think it's a dangerous, stinging insect. But it's just a trick. The moth's look keeps predators away.

Polyphemus Moth

eyespots

RANGE: North America

WINGSPAN: 6 inches (15 cm)

MAGNIFICENT FEATURE: Large, colorful eyespots

Are those feathers? No. They are the antennae of the male Polyphemus moth. The antennae can smell a faraway female.

The Polyphemus moth is mostly orange and tan. The top wings have two tiny spots. The bottom wings have much larger spots. Predators think the spots are eyes. They stay away.

antennae

The rosy maple moth likes yellow! Pink patches cover its yellow wings. Its yellow body is thick—and very fuzzy! The moth rests on hairy pink legs. Its yellow antennae look like feathers. Even its eggs are yellow! Caterpillars are born yellow. They molt and turn green.

caterpillars

RANGE: Parts of the United States and Canada

WINGSPAN: 2 inches (5 cm)

MAGNIFICENT COLORS: Bright pink and yellow

Sunset Moth

RANGE: Madagascar

WINGSPAN: 3.5 inches (8.9 cm)

MAGNIFICENT FEATURE: Black scales look colorful

Don't be fooled! A sunset moth looks colorful. But its wings are all black. Scales on its wings reflect light. The scales trick our eyes into seeing colors. The moth's wings look red, blue, and green. The bright colors send a warning to predators. Stay away!

Spanish **Moon Moth**

female

male

RANGE: Spain and France

WINGSPAN: 4 inches (10 cm)

MAGNIFICENT FEATURES: Eyespots and
long wing tails

Yum! A Spanish moon moth caterpillar
chomps on pine needles. Adults are
nearby. Brown stripes run down their green
wings. Each wing has one eyespot. Males
have long wing tails. Females do not. They
have short, rounded tips instead.

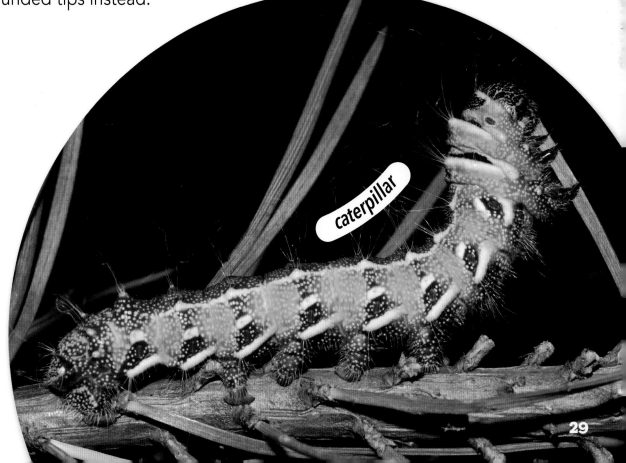

caterpillar

Life Cycle of a Moth

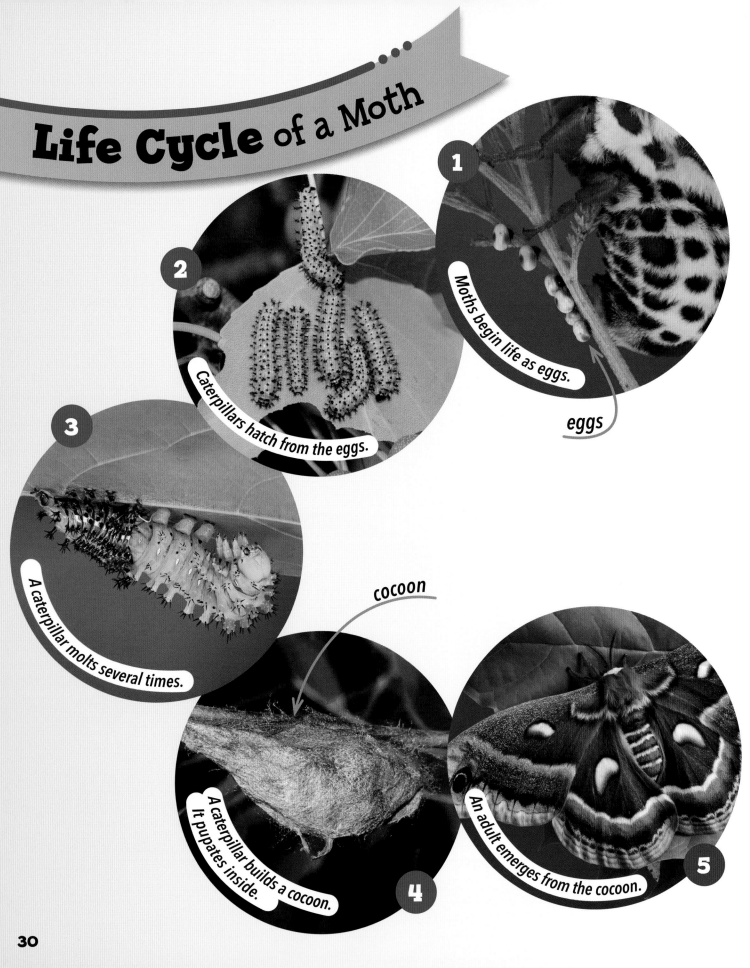

1 Moths begin life as eggs.

eggs

2 Caterpillars hatch from the eggs.

3 A caterpillar molts several times.

cocoon

4 A caterpillar builds a cocoon. It pupates inside.

5 An adult emerges from the cocoon.

Glossary

antenna (an-TEN-uh)—a feeler on an insect's head

camouflage (KA-muh-flahj)—the act of blending in with one's surroundings

caterpillar (KA-tur-pill-uhr)—a larva that changes into a butterfly or moth

cocoon (kuh-KOON)—a covering made of silky thread; insects make a cocoon to protect themselves while they change into adults

feature (FEE-chur)—an important part or quality of something

molt (MOLT)—to shed the hard outer covering while growing

nectar (NEK-tur)—a sweet liquid that some insects collect from flowers and eat as food

predator (PRED-uh-tur)—an animal that hunts another animal for food

pupate (PYOO-peyt)—the process in which an insect changes into an adult

range (RAYNJ)—an area where an animal mostly lives

scale (SKALE)—a small, thin plate that covers the wings of a butterfly or moth

Read More

Carr, Aaron. *Moths.* Fascinating Insects. New York: AV2 by Weigl, 2015.

Herrington, Lisa M. *Butterflies and Moths.* What's the Difference? New York: Children's Press, 2016.

Schuh, Mari. *Moths.* Insect World. Minneapolis: Bullfrog Books, 2015.

Internet Sites

FactHound offers a safe, fun way to find Internet sites related to this book. All of the sites on FactHound have been researched by our staff.

Here's all you do:

Visit *www.facthound.com*

Type in this code: 9781515744993

 Check out projects, games and lots more at **www.capstonekids.com**

Critical Thinking Using the Common Core

1. How many legs do moths have? (Key Idea and Details)

2. Page 27 says the sunset moth has scales. Use the glossary on page 31 to define what a scale is. (Craft and Structure)

3. Choose two moths from the book. How are they alike? How are they different? (Integration of Knowledge and Ideas)

Index